HOW TO MASTER THE ART

OF SALES

Comprehensive Guide To Making Super
Sales

By

Weinberg   Robert

TABLE OF CONTENTS

INTRODUCTION

Defining Sales and Its Pivotal Role in the Business World. Sales can be described as the intersection of supply and demand, the trans-formative conduit through which aspirations materialize into tangible products and services. It's the arena where transactions hold the power to steer entire industries and economies. Let's embark on an expedition into the heart and essence of this captivating and game-changing profession.

Picture a world devoid of sales, a world where groundbreaking ideas remain unnoticed, innovative marvels gather dust and solutions to life's most pressing challenges languish in obscurity. Initiating that inaugural sale stands as a formidable challenge for countless businesses, teeming with myriad questions: "How can I distinguish my product from the competition? How do I gracefully handle objections? What's the art of securing an order?

This short book shows how sales stand as the heartbeat that keeps organizations alive and thriving. Welcome to "Mastering the Art of Sales: A Comprehensive Guide to Success." In this book, we embark on an insightful journey into the captivating world of sales, where ambition meets strategy, and persuasion is an art form. Whether you're a seasoned sales professional aiming to refine your skills or someone who is just starting to explore, this comprehensive guide is designed to equip you with the knowledge, techniques, and mindset needed to excel in this dynamic field.

This book will help you understand that the art of creating a connection is a fundamental component of sales which is frequently undervalued yet has the power to make or break a deal. While many ambitious sales professionals place a heavy emphasis on product knowledge, pitching methods, and closing skills, they frequently ignore the crucial role that interpersonal relationships play in the world of business

CHAPTER 1

UNDERSTANDING SALES FUNDAMENTALS

Navigating The Essentials of Sales

Sales are the lifeblood of any business. Whether you're selling a product, service, or idea, mastering the fundamentals of sales is essential for success. To sell effectively, you must fully understand what you're offering. Be knowledgeable about it features, benefits, and how it solves your customers' problems. This knowledge will build trust with your potential buyers.

and solidify your grounds with your returning buyers. Take your time to understand your customers' needs, preferences, and pain points. Tailor your pitch to address their specific concerns and show how your offering can provide value to them. potential buyers want to be sure they can get what they want and when they want it, and that depends on how you communicate it to them. Listen actively to their questions and concerns, and provide thoughtful answers.

Sales are not just about closing deals or exchanging goods for money, it's about building relationships. Establishing trust and rapport with customers can lead to repeat business and referrals. The journey of growing a business and making sales comes with a lot of rejection, it is part of the sales process. Don't be discouraged by a "no." Instead, view it as an opportunity to learn and improve. closing the deal won't be so difficult if you know your customer, be confident but don't be pushy, and make it easy for the customer to make a decision.

Defining Sales and Its Role in Business: This section should delve into the concept of sales as the process of exchanging goods or services for money and its crucial role in the success of any business. Explain how sales are the lifeblood of an organization, driving revenue and growth.

The Sales Process: A Bird's Eye View: Describe the high-level steps of the sales process, typically consisting of prospecting, preparation, presentation, closing, and follow-up. Emphasize that each step is interconnected and critical to success.

The Psychology of Buying and Selling: Explore the psychology behind buying decisions, including the role of emotions, needs, and desires in the purchasing process. Discuss how understanding these factors can help sales professionals connect with their customers on a deeper level.

Setting Realistic Sales Goals: Explain the importance of setting achievable sales goals and provide strategies for goal-setting, such as using the SMART (Specific, Measurable, Achievable, Relevant, Time-bound) framework.

CHAPTER 2

BUILDING A STRONG SALES FOUNDATION

Forging Sales Excellence And Laying the Cornerstones of Success

A strong sales foundation is the bedrock upon which successful sales efforts are built. Whether you're a seasoned sales professional or just starting in the world of selling, establishing a solid foundation is essential for long-term success. Your journey begins with an in-depth understanding of the product or service you're selling. You should be able to explain its features, benefits, and advantages in a way that resonates with your target audience. It not only instills confidence in potential customers but also allows you to address their specific needs effectively.

You must know your target audience intimately. This means identifying their desires, and motivations. Tailor your sales approach to address these unique aspects, ensuring that your message resonates and offers genuine value. having a good relationship with customers is a long-term investment. Focus on relationship-building rather than quick wins. Engage in honest and transparent interactions, consistently delivering on promises, and showing genuine care for your customers' well-being.

In this current dispensation, sales are made easy with the sales tools and technology available to streamline your efforts. CRM systems, sales analytic, and automation can significantly boost your efficiency and effectiveness.

Here Are Four key Attributes to Consider When Building A Foundation

1. **The Sales Mindset:** Attitude Is Everything: Dive into the importance of having a positive and resilient mindset in sales. Discuss how mindset impacts performance, motivation, and the ability to overcome challenges.

2. **Emotional Intelligence:** Explore the concept of emotional intelligence (EQ) and how it relates to sales success. Provide practical exercises and

techniques for improving EQ, including self-awareness, empathy, and relationship management.

3. **Building Confidence:** Offer tips and strategies for boosting self-confidence, such as mastering product knowledge, practicing sales pitches, and seeking mentor-ship.

4. **Boldness:** Address common fears and challenges faced by sales professionals, such as fear of rejection, and provide practical advice for overcoming these obstacles.

These four key attributes helps you as a sales person especially if you are new to the field

CHAPTER 3

SALES PREPARATION

Sales Mastery Blueprint To Preparing for Success

Sales preparation is the secret ingredient that can transform a good salesperson into a great one. It's the process of equipping yourself with the knowledge, strategies, and mindset needed to engage customers effectively and close deals successfully. Let's delve into why sales preparation is crucial and how to master it.

to be successful as a salesperson, developing a well-thought-out sales strategy helps set clear goals and milestones, and outline your approach for each prospect. Having a structured strategy in place keeps you on track and minimizes the risk of missed opportunities. where most salespersons miss it is when they lack something called presentation skills. these skills, both in terms of content and delivery create engaging and persuasive presentations that highlight the value your product or service offers. Practice your delivery to exude confidence and professionalism.

and do not make the mistake of going to bed just after you finally get that customer, Don't let potential leads slip through the cracks. Develop a follow-up plan to nurture leads and maintain communication. Consistent follow-up can turn your new or prospective customers into loyal customers.

Researching Your Product or Service: Explain the importance of product knowledge and how to conduct adequate research on your offerings. Discuss the benefits of being a subject matter expert.

Understanding Your Target Audience: Explore the process of identifying and segmenting your target audience, including demographics, psycho-graphics, and buying behaviors. Show how this knowledge can inform your sales approach.

Creating a Winning Sales Pitch: Provide a step-by-step guide for crafting a compelling sales pitch that addresses the specific needs and pain points of your prospects. Include examples and templates.

Handling Common Sales Objections: Detail common objections that arise during the sales process and offer strategies for effectively addressing them. Provide rebuttals and responses to objections.

CHAPTER 4

PROSPECTING AND LEAD GENERATION

Prospecting Alchemy, Turning Leads into Gold

In the ever-evolving landscape of sales and marketing, the importance of effective prospecting and lead generation cannot be overstated. These twin pillars serve as the foundation upon which successful customer acquisition and revenue growth are built. In this article, we will explore the nuances of prospecting and lead generation, revealing strategies to make your efforts not only efficient but also genuinely effective.

First, let's clarify the distinction between prospecting and lead generation:

Prospecting: This is the proactive process of identifying and reaching out to potential customers or prospects who have not yet shown explicit interest in your product or service. It involves outbound efforts to create initial contact and gauge interest, such as cold calling, email outreach, and networking.

Lead Generation: Lead generation, on the other hand, involves attracting and capturing the interest of potential customers who have expressed interest in your offering. This interest can be manifested through website visits, downloading resources, subscribing to newsletters, or engaging with your brand on social media.

In other to be effective in prospecting you need to define Your Ideal Customer Profile (ICP) and know the characteristics of the customers who are most likely to benefit from your product or service.

Leverage customer relationship management (CRM) tools and sales automation software to streamline your prospecting efforts.

his content can attract and engage potential leads.

Optimize your website for search engines (SEO) and consider using search engine marketing (SEM) to increase your online visibility and attract organic traffic.

Building and nurturing your email list by sending targeted and valuable content to your subscribers to keep them engaged and informed. your valuable resources, such as e books, webinars, or templates, in exchange for contact information can be an effective way to capture leads.

For maximum success, integrate your prospecting and lead-generation efforts. Leads generated through inbound methods can be further nurtured through outbound prospecting efforts. Ensure that your sales and marketing teams collaborate closely to capitalize on these opportunities.

Identifying Potential Customers: Dive deeper into the process of identifying potential customers, also known as prospects. Discuss techniques for creating customer personas and target profiles to focus your prospecting efforts effectively.

Cold Calling and Warm Calling Techniques: Explain the difference between cold calling (reaching out to prospects who have no prior contact) and warm calling (connecting with prospects who have shown some interest). Provide best practices for both approaches, including script templates and etiquette tips.

Leveraging Social Media for Lead Generation: Discuss the role of social media platforms in modern lead generation and sales. Offer strategies for building a strong online presence, creating engaging content, and using social media to connect with potential customers.

Networking and Building a Referral System: Emphasize the value of networking in sales and provide guidance on how to build a robust network of contacts. Explore the concept of a referral system and how it can lead to high-

quality leads through word-of-mouth marketing.

CHAPTER 5

THE ART OF EFFECTIVE COMMUNICATION

Mastering the Conversation To Unlock Effective Communication

Mastering Verbal and Non-Verbal Communication: Explain the significance of clear and effective communication in sales interactions. Discuss the importance of tone, body language, and voice modulation in conveying confidence and trustworthiness.

Active Listening Skills: Delve into the art of active listening and how it enables sales professionals to understand customer needs and objections better. Provide techniques for active listening, such as paraphrasing and clarifying.

Asking the Right Questions: Discuss the power of asking open-ended questions to engage customers in meaningful conversations. Offer examples of probing questions that can uncover pain points and desires.

Tailoring Your Communication Style: Explore the concept of adaptive communication and how it helps salespeople connect with diverse customer personalities. Provide insights into the DISC personality assessment framework and how it can be applied in sales.

Feel free to continue expanding on the subsequent chapters, adding real-world examples, case studies, and exercises to engage your readers and help them apply the principles you discuss in their sales careers. Each chapter should build upon the previous ones to create a comprehensive guide to mastering the art of sales.

CHAPTER 6

THE SALES PRESENTATION

Captivating Clients And Crafting an Impact Sales Presentation

Structuring a Compelling Sales Presentation: Provide a detailed breakdown of the elements of a successful sales presentation, including the introduction, value proposition, features benefits, and the call to action. Offer templates and tips for creating engaging slide decks or visual aids.

Visual Aids and Multimedia Tools: Discuss the effective use of visuals, multimedia, and technology in sales presentations. Explore how to create impact graphics, videos, and interactive elements to enhance your message.

Storytelling in Sales: Explain the power of storytelling in sales and how it can make your presentation memorable and relatable. Share examples of successful sales stories and guide readers on how to incorporate storytelling into their pitches.

Handling Questions and Objections During the Presentation: Discuss strategies for addressing questions and objections that may arise during your presentation. Offer techniques for maintaining control of the conversation while addressing concerns.

CHAPTER 7

CLOSING THE DEAL

Sealing the Success And The Art of Deal Closure

Recognizing Buying Signals: Teach readers how to recognize signals that indicate a prospect is ready to make a buying decision. Discuss non-verbal cues, verbal cues, and common signs that suggest a close is imminent.

Closing Techniques and Strategies: Provide a comprehensive list of closing techniques, from the assumptive close to the trial close. Explain when and how to use each technique effectively and offer scenarios where they apply.

Overcoming Common Closing Challenges: Explore the common challenges and objections that can arise during the closing phase. Offer specific tactics for overcoming objections, such as price concerns or timing issues.

Setting Up Follow-Up Actions: Stress the importance of post-sale follow-up and relationship building. Guide readers on how to set up follow-up actions, nurture leads, and turn satisfied customers into repeat buyers and advocates.

CHAPTER 8

BUILDING AND MAINTAINING CUSTOMER RELATIONSHIPS

Cultivating Customer Connections Building And sustaining Relationships

The Importance of Customer Relationship Management (CRM): Explain the role of CRM software and systems in managing customer relationships efficiently. Highlight the benefits of organized data and personalized communication.

Providing Exceptional Customer Service: Discuss the correlation between outstanding customer service and long-term customer relationships. Offer strategies for exceeding customer expectations and resolving issues effectively.

Post-Sale Relationship Building: Show readers how to continue building relationships after the sale, including strategies for up-selling, cross-selling, and maintaining open lines of communication.

Turning Customers into Advocates: Explore the concept of turning satisfied customers into brand advocates and promoters. Discuss strategies for creating referral programs and encouraging customers to share their positive experiences

CHAPTER 9

SALES ETHICS AND INTEGRITY

Ethical Selling, The Heart of Trustworthy Sales Practices

The Role of Ethics in Sales: Emphasize the importance of ethical behavior in sales and how it contributes to long-term success. Discuss the potential consequences of unethical sales practices.

Common Ethical Dilemmas in Sales: Explore real-world ethical dilemmas that sales professionals may face, such as pressure to meet quotas, truth in advertising, and conflicts of interest. Guide how to navigate these situations ethically.

Maintaining Integrity in the Sales Process: Offer practical tips and strategies for maintaining integrity throughout the entire sales process, from prospecting to closing and beyond.

The Long-Term Benefits of Ethical Selling: Highlight the long-term benefits of ethical selling, including trust, reputation, and customer loyalty. Show readers how ethical behavior can lead to a sustainable and fulfilling sales career.

CHAPTER 10

MEASURING AND IMPROVING SALES
PERFORMANCE

Elevating Excellence: Metrics and Strategies for Sales
Performance Improvement

Key Sales Metrics and KPIs: Introduce readers to
essential sales metrics and key performance indicators
(KPIs) that help measure sales effectiveness. Discuss
how tracking metrics can inform sales strategies.

Using Data to Enhance Sales Strategies: Explain how
data analysis can provide insights into customer behavior,

market trends, and sales performance. Provide examples of tools and techniques for data-driven decision-making.

Continuous Learning and Professional Development: Emphasize the importance of ongoing learning and development in the sales profession. Discuss the value of sales training, workshops, and mentor-ship programs.

Adapting to Changing Market Conditions: Explore how sales professionals can adapt to evolving market conditions, emerging technologies, and shifts in consumer behavior. Guide staying agile and proactive in the face of change.

CONCLUSION

As you near the end of your journey through "Mastering the Art of Sales," it's essential to reflect on the key takeaways from this comprehensive guide. Throughout the preceding chapters, you've explored the intricate world of sales, from its fundamental principles to advanced techniques. Let's revisit some of the pivotal lessons you've encountered:

You've learned that sales are not merely about transactions; it's about building relationships, solving problems, and creating value for both customers and organizations.

The importance of a positive sales mindset, emotional intelligence, and confidence in establishing trust and credibility with your prospects and customers has been emphasized.

Sales preparation, including in-depth research, understanding your target audience, and crafting compelling sales pitches, is the foundation upon which successful sales interactions are built.

The art of effective communication, encompassing verbal and non-verbal skills, active listening, and the ability to ask the right questions, has been unveiled as a critical aspect of sales excellence.

In the sales presentation phase, you've discovered how to structure persuasive pitches, harness visual aids, tell compelling stories, and effectively handle objections.

The closing of a deal, a culmination of the sales process, involves recognizing buying signals, using various closing techniques, and navigating objections with finesse.

Beyond the transaction, this guide has shown you how to build and maintain long-lasting customer relationships, providing exceptional customer service and turning customers into advocates.

Ethical considerations in sales, from transparency and honesty to maintaining integrity throughout the sales process, have been thoroughly explored.

Lastly, you've learned the importance of measuring and improving sales performance, using key metrics, data-driven decision-making, continuous learning, and adaptability to stay competitive in an ever-evolving market.

Your Journey as a Sales Professional

As you absorb these lessons and strategies, remember that your journey as a sales professional is a dynamic and ongoing process. Sales is not a destination; it's a continuous voyage of growth and discovery. The skills and knowledge you've acquired within these pages serve as a strong foundation upon which you can build a successful and fulfilling career in sales.

Encouragement and Final Thoughts

In closing, always remember that success in sales is not solely measured by numbers or quotas but by the impact you make on the lives of your customers. Approach your work with a genuine desire to help others, and success will naturally follow.

Embrace rejection as an opportunity to learn and grow, and let it fuel your determination to improve. Seek out mentors and colleagues who can provide guidance and support along the way.

The world of sales is ever-evolving, and as you continue to hone your skills, stay adaptable, open to change, and committed to your personal and professional development.

You now possess the knowledge, tools, and mindset needed to navigate the complex and rewarding terrain of sales. With dedication, practice, and a commitment to ethical conduct, you have the potential to not only excel but to thrive in this dynamic field.

Your journey as a masterful sales professional awaits. As you step forward, know that you have the ability to create meaningful connections, solve problems, and contribute to the success of your organization while achieving your own goals. Embrace the art of sales, and may your career be filled with countless victories, lasting relationships, and a profound sense of fulfillment

www.ingramcontent.com/pod-product-compliance
Lightning Source LLC
Chambersburg PA
CBHW062301290526
45794CB00006B/2647

* 9 7 9 8 8 6 1 5 7 1 1 2 8 *